My Singing Monsters
Official Handbook

EGMONT
We bring stories to life

First published in Great Britain in 2015 by Egmont UK Ltd,
The Yellow Building, 1 Nicholas Road, London W11 4AN

Written by Katrina Pallant. Designed by Anthony Duke.

ISBN 978 1 4052 7685 6
59697/1
Printed in China

Contents

WELCOME TO THE WORLD OF MY SINGING MONSTERS! A magical, musical place where you can grow your own band of singing creatures, design amazing islands and create a symphony like nothing you've ever heard!

Inside this handbook you will find all you need to know about the musical creatures of PLANT, COLD, AIR, WATER AND EARTH ISLANDS, plus what happens on the mysterious GOLD, SHUGABUSH AND ETHEREAL ISLANDS. Ace your game with top secret tips from the monster-handlers, the makers of the app.

This handbook will take you through the gameplay of the app, and introduce you to a few monsters you may not have met yet! This is the ultimate guide to MY SINGING MONSTERS and includes information you won't find anywhere else!

Find bonus features using the Blippar app whenever you see this symbol:

DOWNLOAD
BLIPPAR

FILL SCREEN
with image

BLIPP IMAGE
into life!

Getting Started

If you're already a **MY SiNGiNG MONSTeRS** player, you can skip this page! If not, here's how to get started.

You can download the app for free from your favourite app store onto your phone or tablet. The default login method is 'Anonymous' – if you want to transfer your progress, you can always bind your account to an email address. From there, you can access your account via email from any phone or tablet!

The Essential Guide

In this handbook you will find profiles for each monster. Here are the essentials you need to know to understand them.

SPECIES: Each monster has its own species name. You can give each monster a unique name too.

EGG: This is what each monster will hatch from. When breeding, this helps you identify the monster you have created, so you know if you have been successful.

UNLOCKED: Not all monsters are available from the beginning of the game. You will have to work through your goals gaining experience points to reach the later level monsters.

ISLANDS: Some monsters are only available on certain islands, due to their Elements or breeding patterns.

BEDS REQUIRED:  Each island has a Castle that holds a certain numbers of beds. You must have enough to hold each monster you want to place. You can obtain extra beds by buying a Hotel structure.

BREEDING/INCUBATION TIME: If you are trying to breed a monster instead of buying it from the Market you have to wait for it to be ready in the Breeding Structure. Some monsters take longer than others.

ELEMENTS: Each monster is made up of one to four Elements. These are important for knowing which island they can live on and how to breed them. To find out more about Elements see page 24.

CLASS: Elements are divided into Classes, whose Elements share the same breeding behaviors.

PLACEMENT 🌟XP: This is how many experience points you will gain from placing your monster on an island. So, even if you want to sell a monster straight after it has hatched, it is still worthwhile to place it first.

LIKES: These relate to your monsters' Happiness. See page 16 for more information.

HOW TO BREED: There are lots of different ways to breed each monster; this is just one of them. See page 17 for the basic information.

Plant Island

You will begin your adventure on **PLANT ISLAND**. The other islands will become available as you progress. Plant Island is a **SERENE, SLEEPY PLACE**, with sounds of nature filling the air. It won't stay peaceful for long – as you start to add monsters and structures, the island becomes a very noisy place indeed! The monsters that live on Plant Island produce a **CHEERFUL AND CATCHY** tune.

Monsters on this island are of the **EARTH, PLANT, WATER AND COLD ELEMENTS**. No **AIR** Element monsters can live on this island, so you cannot breed them here or purchase them from the Market.

PLANT ISLAND'S CASTLE: Every island comes with a Basic Castle. To start with the Castle only has **4 BEDS**, but using your currency you will need to upgrade the Castle to get **ENOUGH BEDS FOR ALL YOUR MONSTERS**. Once upgraded, the Castle produces a bass sound.

Each island has **OBSTACLES IN PLACE** when you first access them. These are the Plant Island obstacles:

SMALL ROCK

COST: 500 ©
XP ⭐: 500
CLEAR-TIME: 10 mins
UNLOCKED: Level 4

MEDIUM ROCK

COST: 10,000 ©
XP ⭐: 10,000
CLEAR-TIME: 8 hrs
UNLOCKED: Level 6

BIG ROCK

COST: 15,000 ©
XP ⭐: 15,000
CLEAR-TIME: 12 hrs
UNLOCKED: Level 6

SMALL TREE

COST: 100 ©
XP ⭐: 100
CLEAR-TIME: 20 secs
UNLOCKED: Level 4

MEDIUM TREE

COST: 1,000 ©
XP ⭐: 1,000
CLEAR-TIME: 2 hrs
UNLOCKED: Level 5

BIG TREE

COST: 2,500 ©
XP ⭐: 2,500
CLEAR-TIME: 4 hrs
UNLOCKED: Level 5

CLEARING THESE AWAY will not only give you more room for your monsters, but also help you gain **EXPERIENCE POINTS.**

Meet the Noggin!

You can only get the **NOGGIN** from the Market — so first you will have to purchase an egg. The egg will appear in the Nursery and take 15 seconds to hatch. When your Noggin has hatched you can place it anywhere you like on Plant Island.

Noggins are basically musical rocks. They add a **STEADY BEAT** to the island song by **SLAPPING THEIR FLAT HEADS** with their enormous hands. The sensation of reverberation produced by a Noggin motivates all other monsters.

SPECIES: Noggin

EGG:

UNLOCKED: Level 1

ISLANDS: Plant, Air, Water, Earth and Gold

BEDS REQUIRED: 1

BREEDING/INCUBATION TIME: 15 seconds

ELEMENT: Earth

CLASS: Natural

PLACEMENT XP: 150

LIKES:

HOW TO BREED: Initially, Noggins can only be purchased from the Market, but breeding of a Noggin with another monster can also produce a Noggin.

Goals

Once you have placed the Noggin you will have **COMPLETED YOUR FIRST GOAL AND CAN COLLECT YOUR REWARD.** The goals will guide you through the basics of creating your monster band, adding structures and decorations, and the essentials to gain points and progress through the levels. You will be given **a REWARD OF COINS, FOOD, DIAMONDS OR EXPERIENCE POINTS** for every goal you complete.

Meet the Mammott!

Buy it from the Market and add it to your island to join your Noggin. Don't forget to give it its own unique name!

MAMMOTTS produce a **DEEP BELLOWING** sound, providing a bass line to the islands. They have luxurious fur ensuring the cold does not get to them. Their resonant anthem celebrates blizzards and frosted windows.

SPECIES: Mammott

EGG:

UNLOCKED: Level 2

ISLANDS: Plant, Cold, Air, Earth and Gold

BEDS REQUIRED: 1

BREEDING/INCUBATION TIME: 2 minutes

ELEMENT: Cold

CLASS: Natural

PLACEMENT : 150

LIKES:

HOW TO BREED: Initially, Mammotts can only be purchased from the Market, but breeding of a Mammott with another monster can also produce a Mammott.

Mini Games: Scratch Ticket

Mini games like the Scratch Ticket reward players who visit the monster world every day! Each Ticket is a winner, and when you match three squares of the same prize, it's yours to collect! You can choose to play the Scratch Ticket more than once by using your diamonds. There's also a special weekly Monster Scratch Ticket in the Nursery, which gives you a chance to win a monster egg!

Dinner Time

To help your monsters achieve higher levels of earning and breeding, you need to feed them! Food can be made in the **BAKERY**. To place a bakery, head to the Market and look in the structures section. How much food you can bake depends on the size of the bakery — you can start with a **SMALL BAKERY** and upgrade it later.

You have to feed a monster **4 TIMES** before it will level up.

SMALL BAKERY

Cupcakes		50	+ 30 seconds = **5 UNITS**
Cookies		250	+ 5 minutes = **25 UNITS**
Bread		1,000	+ 30 minutes = **100 UNITS**

MEDIUM BAKERY

As per small bakery plus:

Donuts		5,000	+ 1 hour = **500 UNITS**
Ice cream		15,000	+ 3 hours = **1,500 UNITS**
Pizza		75,000	+ 6 hours = **7,500 UNITS**

LARGE BAKERY

As per small and medium bakery plus:

Pies		500,000	+ 12 hours = **50,000 UNITS**
Turkey		1,000,000	+ 24 hours = **100,000 UNITS**
Cake		5,000,000	+ 48 hours = **500,000 UNITS**

Meet the Toe Jammer!

Buy a **TOe JaMMeR** egg from the Market and place it with your growing band.

Toe Jammers produce a **DOO-WAH** sound perfectly complementing the Mammott's bellow. They sing of deep sea leviathans, crashing surf and bubble tea!

SPECIES: Toe Jammer

EGG:

UNLOCKeD: Level 4

ISLaNDS: Plant, Cold, Air, Water and Gold

BeDS ReQuiReD: 1

BReeDiNG/iNCuBATiON TiMe: 1 minute

ELeMeNT: Water

CLASS: Natural

PLaCeMeNT XP: 125

LiKeS:

HOW TO BReeD: Initially, Toe Jammers can only be purchased from the Market, but breeding of a Toe Jammer with another monster can also produce a Toe Jammer.

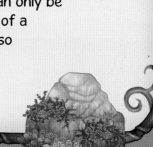

Happiness

How quickly a monster makes COiNS depends on how happy it is. If you select one of your monsters and tap on the Info button, you can open the LiKeS tab. This will tell you which decorations and other monsters make your monster happy. As you place each object next to your monster LiTTLe HeaRTS will appear and its Happiness will go up by 25%. Monsters reach full earning potential when they are at 100% Happiness. A monster's final Like is hidden (indicated by the question mark in the monster profiles), so you need to eXPeRiMeNT by moving items and monsters around to find it! Monsters liked by each monster can vary from island to island, so we have left those up to you to find as well.

Breeding – the Basics

Now that you have a few monsters you can start **BREEDING**. You will need a Breeding Structure, which you can buy in the Market. Each monster must be at **LEVEL 4 OR HIGHER** in order to breed so don't forget to feed them! Have a go at combining the monsters on your island to see what you come up with! Once the egg is ready transfer it to the Nursery to hatch.

BREEDING STRUCTURE

NURSERY

TOP TIP!
Breeding higher level monsters together increases your chances of getting a **SPECIAL MONSTER!**

Meet the Drumpler!

Once you have successfully bred a **DRUMPLER** you can add its **CONTINUOUS DRUMMING** to your band.

The Drumpler's tough abdominal hide can be stretched taut to produce sound as it taps its drumsticks across it, yet the Drumpler experiences no discomfort whatsoever.

SPECIES: Drumpler

EGG:

UNLOCKED: Level 7

ISLANDS: Plant, Air, Earth and Gold

BEDS REQUIRED: 2

BREEDING/INCUBATION TIME: 30 minutes

ELEMENTS: Earth and Cold

CLASS: Natural

PLACEMENT : 2,125

LIKES:

HOW TO BREED: Once you have fed your Mammott and Noggin so that they reach Level 4, they are ready to breed. Pair these two creatures to create the scaly Drumpler.

Meet the Maw!

After successfully breeding the Maw, add some colour to the landscape with this bright pink, melodic monster.

The Maw sings 'Dee-Dee-Dee' over the top of the other monsters. It is a very distinctive sound so you won't have trouble locating it in a crowd.

SPECIES: Maw

EGG:

UNLOCKED: Level 7

ISLANDS: Plant, Cold, Air and Gold

BEDS REQUIRED: 2

BREEDING/INCUBATION TIME: 30 minutes

ELEMENTS: Water and Cold

CLASS: Natural

PLACEMENT XP: 2,125

LIKES:

HOW TO BREED: Feed your Toe Jammer so that it reaches Level 4 and then pair it with your Mammott in the Breeding Structure. You should successfully breed a furry Maw!

Meet the Fwog!

The **FWOG** is a frog-like wonder, passionately singing in the hope of attracting a companion. Once you have successfully bred this monster, its **HYPNOTIC CALL** will fill the air, exciting all the other monsters on your island.

SPECIES: Fwog

EGG:

UNLOCKED: Level 7

ISLANDS: Plant, Air, Water and Gold

BEDS REQUIRED: 2

BREEDING/INCUBATION TIME: 30 minutes

ELEMENTS: Earth and Water

CLASS: Natural

PLACEMENT : 2,125

LIKES:

HOW TO BREED: Take your Level 4 Noggin and your Level 4 Toe Jammer and pair up to breed a big-lipped Fwog.

Visiting Friends

One of your first goals is to add a friend who also has the **MY SINGING MONSTERS APP** installed. You can do this by going to the **FRIENDS MENU** and selecting 'Invite Friends' then selecting how you would like to connect with them. **FRIEND CODES** can be found in the Options menu under **HELP**. Once you have added your friends you can visit their islands on your device any time you like. You can also **RATE THEIR ISLANDS**. In the Friends menu you will also see that you can visit random islands, so you can view and rate what other people are doing.

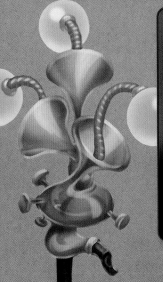

Island Rankings

In the Friends menu you will see that you can visit the **TOP RANKED ISLANDS**. These are the islands that have been given the most likes when viewed by other players. To **GAIN MORE LIKES** yourself, experiment with decorations, placement of monsters and sound. To add a personal touch, you can adjust the tempo of each island's song using the special **TIME MACHINE** structure.

TOP TIP!
Mute specific monsters or add multiples to **VARY THE SOUND** of your island.

Meet the T-Rox!

The **T-ROX** exudes enthusiasm and energy, displaying flashing spikelets and chomping jaws. It provides a **SYNTHESIZED DRUMMING** by pounding its feet and snapping its jaw.

SPECIES: T-Rox

EGG:

UNLOCKED: Level 7

ISLANDS: Plant, Air and Gold

BEDS REQUIRED: 3

BREEDING/INCUBATION TIME: 8 hours

ELEMENTS: Earth, Water and Cold

CLASS: Natural

PLACEMENT : 8,000

LIKES:

HOW TO BREED: Because the T-Rox is a Triple-Element monster, it can be bred using more than just one combination of monsters. Any combination of Earth, Water and Cold Elements should result in a successful breeding of the T-Rox. The Maw and the Noggin are one combination you could use because the Maw has both Cold and Water, and the Noggin has the Earth Element. See if you can find some other ways of doing it.

Breeding –
Using the Natural Elements

The Natural Elements in the game are:

PLANT

COLD

AIR

WATER

EARTH

Each monster can be made up of one, two, three or four of these Elements.

SiNGLE-ELEMENT MONSTERS can only be bought from the Market in the first instance.

As we've seen with the T-Rox you need to breed two monsters with the corresponding Elements to get **MULTiPLE-ELEMENT MONSTERS**. It is important to remember that if an Element is repeated in a combination, the breeding outcome is guaranteed to be one of the original monsters, not a new monster.

Even when you are using the correct combination, breeding is not successful 100% of the time. Complex combinations involving monster of two or more Elements each can be unstable and may turn out like a parent. You might have to try more than once to get the monster you want.

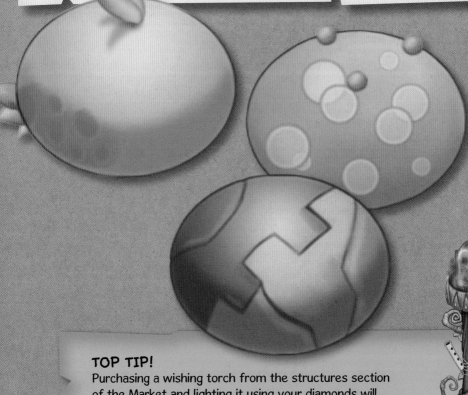

TOP TIP!
Purchasing a wishing torch from the structures section of the Market and lighting it using your diamonds will increase the chances that your breeding attempts will be successful. The more torches the better!

Meet the Potbelly!

The **POTBELLY**, the most mischievous of all the plant monsters, can **GROW LIKE WEEDS** if ever allowed out of their pots. Your islands aren't complete without these **HARMONISING** heads.

SPECIES: Potbelly

EGG:

UNLOCKED: Level 9

ISLANDS: Plant, Cold, Water, Earth and Gold

BEDS REQUIRED: 1

BREEDING/INCUBATION TIME: 2 hours

ELEMENT: Plant

CLASS: Natural

PLACEMENT : 125

LIKES:

HOW TO BREED: Initially, Potbellies can only be purchased from the Market, but breeding of a Potbelly with another monster can also produce a Potbelly.

Meet the Shrubb!

The **SHRUBB** is constantly moving, even when it isn't making any sound. Some consider this to be a graceful ballet. The tall, bush-like creature **BEATBOXES** helping with the **STEADY BEAT** of the chorus.

SPECIES: Shrubb

EGG:

UNLOCKED: Level 9

ISLANDS: Plant, Water, Earth and Gold

BEDS REQUIRED: 2

BREEDING/INCUBATION TIME: 8 hours

ELEMENTS: Plant and Earth

CLASS: Natural

PLACEMENT : 4,000

LIKES:

HOW TO BREED: To create this Double-Element monster, you will need both a Single-Element Plant monster and a Single-Element Earth monster. Try the Noggin and Potbelly combo!

Meet the Oaktopus!

The **OAKTOPUS** has a low raspy voice producing a subtle song. Its roots are actually powerful tentacles that carry the Oaktopus rapidly across landscapes and propel it efficiently through water.

SPECIES: Oaktopus

EGG:

UNLOCKED: Level 9

ISLANDS: Plant, Cold, Water and Gold

BEDS REQUIRED: 2

BREEDING/INCUBATION TIME: 8 hours

ELEMENTS: Plant and Water

CLASS: Natural

PLACEMENT : 4,000

LIKES:

HOW TO BREED: To create this Plant and Water Element monster, you will need both a Single-Element plant monster and a Single-Element water monster. Make sure both your Toe Jammer and Potbelly are at Level 4!

 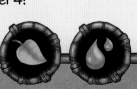

Meet the Furcorn!

These special creatures contribute a **HIGH WARBLE** to the island song. They are **TINY** and delicate, but maintain a steady internal temperature by fluffing or flattening their silky green pelt. These cute green monsters need protecting, so it's good to keep them in groups.

SPECIES: Furcorn

EGG:

UNLOCKED: Level 9

ISLANDS: Plant, Cold, Earth and Gold

BEDS REQUIRED: 2

BREEDING/INCUBATION TIME: 8 hours

ELEMENTS: Plant and Cold

CLASS: Natural

PLACEMENT ⭐: 4,000

LIKES:

HOW TO BREED: To create this Plant and Cold Element monster, you will need both a Single-Element Plant monster and a Single-Element Cold monster. Pair up a Potbelly and a Mammott!

Meet the Bowgart!

The **BOWGART** acts as both the upper and lower string section of an orchestra. Its four arms mean it can play a **COMPLICATED MELODY** on its string instrument. The Bowgart loves to stand in puddles, sucking up the muddy mixture to feed the rapid growth of its horns, which in turn replace its instrument once shed.

SPECIES: Bowgart

EGG:

UNLOCKED: Level 9

ISLANDS: Plant, Cold and Gold

BEDS REQUIRED: 3

BREEDING/INCUBATION TIME: 12 hours

ELEMENTS: Plant, Water and Cold

CLASS: Natural

PLACEMENT XP: 10,000

LIKES:

HOW TO BREED: Any combination of Plant, Water and Cold monsters. Try pairing the Oaktopus and the Mammott.

Meet the Pummel!

The **PUMMEL**'s contribution to the island's song is a **POUNDING DRUM SOUND**. Its two tongues end in orbs that beat rhythmically on the plant membrane stretched over its mouth. Pummels are closely in tune with the Earth, but are aquatic and breathe through gills.

SPECIES: Pummel

EGG:

UNLOCKED: Level 9

ISLANDS: Plant, Water and Gold

BEDS REQUIRED: 3

BREEDING/INCUBATION TIME: 12 hours

ELEMENTS: Plant, Earth and Water

CLASS: Natural

PLACEMENT : 10,000

LIKES:

HOW TO BREED: Any combination of Plant, Earth and Water Element creatures should result in a Pummel. Try to find some for yourself, but if you get stuck pairing the Potbelly and the Fwog should produce results.

Meet the Clamble!

The **CLAMBLE** produces a **CYMBAL SOUND** by beating its two head plates together and tapping the plate in its hand. As it grows it saves the cast-off plates from its head to add to its sound.

SPECIES: Clamble

EGG:

UNLOCKED: Level 9

ISLANDS: Plant, Earth and Gold

BEDS REQUIRED: 3

BREEDING/INCUBATION TIME: 12 hours

ELEMENTS: Plant, Earth and Cold

CLASS: Natural

PLACEMENT : 10,000

LIKES:

HOW TO BREED: Any combination of Plant, Earth and Cold Element monsters. One example is to pair the Potbelly and the Drumpler, but there are others.

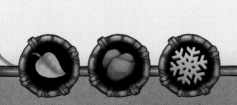

32

Meet the Entbrat!

The **ENTBRAT** is a gentle giant whose **GREAT BELLOW** vibrates across the whole Plant Island. It sways back and forth to the rhythm of the island's song.

SPECIES: Entbrat

EGG:

UNLOCKED: Level 9

ISLANDS: Plant and Gold

BEDS REQUIRED: 4

BREEDING/INCUBATION TIME: 24 hours

ELEMENTS: Plant, Earth, Water and Cold

CLASS: Natural

PLACEMENT : 110,000

Likes:

HOW TO BREED: The Entbrat is the 'boss' of the Plant Island, meaning it is made of Plant Island's four Elements – Plant, Earth, Water and Cold. To breed a Quad-Element monster you can combine a pair of Double-Element monsters – for an Entbrat try pairing a Shrubb and a Maw – but you may have more success with a combination of a Single-Element monster and a Triple-Element monster. Try pairing the Clamble and the Toe Jammer for this Plant boss.

Cold Island

COLD ISLAND is available for purchase at Level 4 for 200,000 Coins. It is a **BLEAK AND LONELY PLACE** until the winter festival of monsters arrives!

Monsters on this island are of the **AIR, PLANT, WATER AND COLD ELEMENTS.** No **EARTH** Element monsters can live on this island, so you cannot breed them here or purchase them from the Market.

These are the Cold Island obstacles:

SMALL ROCK	**MEDIUM ROCK**	**BIG ROCK**
COST: 1,000 ⓒ	**COST:** 15,000 ⓒ	**COST:** 50,000 ⓒ
XP ⭐: 1,000	**XP** ⭐: 15,000	**XP** ⭐: 50,000
CLEAR-TIME: 2 hrs	**CLEAR-TIME:** 12 hrs	**CLEAR-TIME:** 16 hrs
UNLOCKED: after buying island	**UNLOCKED:** after buying island	**UNLOCKED:** after buying island

SMALL TREE	**MEDIUM TREE**	**BIG TREE**
COST: 500 ⓒ	**COST:** 2,500 ⓒ	**COST:** 10,000 ⓒ
XP ⭐: 500	**XP** ⭐: 2,500	**XP** ⭐: 10,000
CLEAR-TIME: 10 mins	**CLEAR-TIME:** 4 hrs	**CLEAR-TIME:** 8 hrs
UNLOCKED: after buying island	**UNLOCKED:** after buying island	**UNLOCKED:** after buying island

Meet the Tweedle!

The **TWEEDLE** is a flighty songbird who loves to fly around spreading gossip and secrets. Its **HIGH-PITCHED MELODY** livens up any island.

SPECIES: Tweedle

EGG:

UNLOCKED: Level 4

ISLANDS: Cold, Air, Water, Earth and Gold

BEDS REQUIRED: 1

BREEDING/INCUBATION TIME: 4 hours

ELEMENT: Air

CLASS: Natural

PLACEMENT : 150

LIKES:

HOW TO BREED: Initially, Tweedles can only be purchased from the Market, but breeding of a Tweedle with another monster can also produce a Tweedle.

Adding Core Monsters for Breeding

When you start a new island you will need to purchase **SINGLE-ELEMENT MONSTERS** to help you breed your residents. **THERE ARE FIVE CORE NATURAL MONSTERS:**

THE NOGGIN

THE MAMMOTT

THE TOE JAMMER

THE POTBELLY

THE TWEEDLE

Of course, as you already know, not all of these can appear on every island, but you will need the four allowed monsters on every island for successful breeding.

You will also need to breed all of these together to get the Double-Element monsters needed for the more complicated Triple and Quad-Element monsters.

Meet the Dandidoo!

The DANDIDOO has a tail and hair that resemble dandelion tufts and likes to strut elegantly around the landscape CHIRPING A JOYFUL TUNE.

SPECIES: Dandidoo

EGG:

UNLOCKED: After buying Cold Island

ISLANDS: Cold, Water, Earth and Gold

BEDS REQUIRED: 2

BREEDING/INCUBATION TIME: 8 hours

ELEMENTS: Air and Plant

CLASS: Natural

PLACEMENT XP: 4,000

LIKES:

HOW TO BREED: To create this Plant and Air Element monster, you will need both a Single-Element Plant monster and a Single-Element Air monster.
Pair up a Tweedle and a Potbelly!

Meet the Quibble!

QUIBBLES collect resonant rocks that they use to build their keyboards, but only when the two Quibble minds are able to agree on a single purpose. The Quibble's contribution to an island's song is the SOUND OF A PIANO. Each head is responsible for playing the note on its own side of the instrument.

SPECIES: Quibble

EGG:

UNLOCKED: After buying Cold Island

ISLANDS: Cold, Air, Water and Gold

BEDS REQUIRED: 2

BREEDING/INCUBATION TIME: 8 hours

ELEMENTS: Air and Water

CLASS: Natural

PLACEMENT XP: 4,000

LIKES:

HOW TO BREED: Take your Level 4 Tweedle and Level 4 Toe Jammer and combine to make this musical two-headed bird.

Meet the Pango!

This flightless bird-like monster is **PERPETUALLY CHILLY**. It remains on the ground chattering its beak and shivering, producing a **CASTANET-LIKE** sound.

SPECIES: Pango

EGG:

UNLOCKED: After buying Cold Island

ISLANDS: Cold, Air, Water and Gold

BEDS REQUIRED: 2

BREEDING/INCUBATION TIME: 8 hours

ELEMENTS: Air and Cold

CLASS: Natural

PLACEMENT XP: 4,000

LIKES:

HOW TO BREED: To create this Air and Cold Element monster, you will need both a Single-Element Air monster and a Single-Element Cold monster. Try the Tweedle and Mammott combo!

Meet the Spunge!

The **SPUNGE WHISTLES** by filling up with air, but this mischievous lump also likes to fill up with water and **SPURT IT** at unsuspecting bystanders.

SPECIES: Spunge

EGG:

UNLOCKED: After buying Cold Island

ISLANDS: Cold, Water and Gold

BEDS REQUIRED: 3

BREEDING/INCUBATION TIME: 12 hours

ELEMENTS: Air, Plant and Water

CLASS: Natural

PLACEMENT XP: 11,000

LIKES:

HOW TO BREED: Any combination of Air, Plant and Water Element creatures should result in a Spunge. Try to find some for yourself, but if you get stuck pairing the Tweedle and the Oaktopus should produce results.

Meet the Thumpies!

The **THUMPIES** come in sets of two. These fun monsters bounce on mushrooms and a tree stump to create their **THUMPING MELODY**.

SPECIES: Thumpies

EGG:

UNLOCKED: After buying Cold Island

ISLANDS: Cold, Earth and Gold

BEDS REQUIRED: 3

BREEDING/INCUBATION TIME: 12 hours

ELEMENTS: Air, Plant and Cold

CLASS: Natural

PLACEMENT XP: 11,000

LIKES:

HOW TO BREED: Any combination of Air, Plant and Cold monsters. Try pairing the Furcorn and the Tweedle.

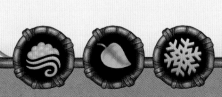

Meet the Congle!

After the **CONGLE** hatches, it recycles the egg and uses it as a drum. It also uses all the other monsters' eggs too. The **CONGLE'S STEADY BEAT** leads the island in a conga-like song.

SPECIES: Congle

EGG:

UNLOCKED: After buying Cold Island

ISLANDS: Cold, Air and Gold

BEDS REQUIRED: 3

BREEDING/INCUBATION TIME: 12 hours

ELEMENTS: Air, Water and Cold

CLASS: Natural

PLACEMENT XP: 11,000

LIKES:

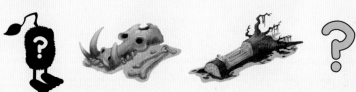

HOW TO BREED: Any combination of Air, Cold and Water Element monsters. One example is to pair the Toe Jammer and the Pango, but there are others.

Meet the Deedge!

The **DEEDGE** keeps all the monsters on Cold Island dancing with its tireless energy. The **DEEDGE** produces a **RHYTHMIC BEAT** like a DJ by striking large ice blocks, amplified through a pair of speakers.

SPECIES: Deedge

EGG:

UNLOCKED: After buying Cold Island

ISLANDS: Cold and Gold

BEDS REQUIRED: 4

BREEDING/INCUBATION TIME: 24 hours

ELEMENTS: Air, Plant, Water and Cold

CLASS: Natural

PLACEMENT XP: 110,000

LIKES:

HOW TO BREED: The Deedge is the 'boss' of the Cold Island, meaning it is made of the four Cold Island Elements – Plant, Cold, Water and Air. Combine a Double-Element monster pair like the Dandidoo and Maw, or for more stability try a Triple-Element and Single-Element combo, like the Spunge and Mammott.

Mini Games: Memory Game

The memory game is accessible in the Castle once you have 4 monsters on your island. When you enter the game you have to select 4 monsters to play with. You then have to copy whatever those monsters do. The longer the sequence you remember the better. If you beat your personal best, you win diamonds! You can play more than once a day by using your diamonds.

Air Island

AiR ISLaND is available for purchase for 750,000 Coins, but only after you have purchased COLD ISLaND. Air Island is ready for a party in the clouds. Once the monsters have arrived there will be all manner of SHENANiGaNS with dancing and singing to its FUNKY TUNe!

Monsters on this island are of the AiR, EARTH, WaTER aND COLD ELeMeNTS. No PLaNT Element monsters can live on this island, so you cannot breed them here or purchase them from the Market.

These are the Air Island obstacles:

SMALL ROCK

COST: 2,500
XP: 2,500
CLEAR-TIME: 4 hrs
UNLOCKED: after buying island

MEDIUM ROCK

COST: 50,000
XP: 50,000
CLEAR-TIME: 16 hrs
UNLOCKED: after buying island

BIG ROCK

COST: 75,000
XP: 75,000
CLEAR-TIME: 20 hrs
UNLOCKED: after buying island

SMALL TREE

COST: 1,000
XP: 1,000
CLEAR-TIME: 2 hrs
UNLOCKED: after buying island

MEDIUM TREE

COST: 10,000
XP: 10,000
CLEAR-TIME: 8 hrs
UNLOCKED: after buying island

BIG TREE

COST: 15,000
XP: 15,000
CLEAR-TIME: 12 hrs
UNLOCKED: after buying island

Meet the Cybop!

The **CYBOP** is more than a mere **GIZMO**; it is a vibrant addition to any island it is on. It has a propeller on its head and a large metal jaw, both of which help to produce the **ROBOTIC MELODY** that vibrates around the land.

SPECIES: Cybop

EGG:

UNLOCKED: After buying Air Island

ISLANDS: Air, Water, Earth and Gold

BEDS REQUIRED: 2

BREEDING/INCUBATION TIME: 8 hours

ELEMENTS: Air and Earth

CLASS: Natural

PLACEMENT XP: 4,000

LIKES:

HOW TO BREED: To create this Air and Earth Element monster, you will need both a Single-Element Air monster and a Single-Element Earth monster. Pair up a Tweedle and a Noggin!

Meet the PomPom!

The **POMPOM** grows its brilliant pink plumes by eating only red food. Your islands are not complete without this enthusiastic cheerleader. Its **UPLIFTING CRY** is accompanied by an eye-catching dance.

SPECIES: PomPom

EGG:

UNLOCKED: After buying Air Island

ISLANDS: Air, Earth, and Gold

BEDS REQUIRED: 3

BREEDING/INCUBATION TIME: 12 hours

ELEMENTS: Air, Earth and Cold

CLASS: Natural

PLACEMENT XP: 11,000

LIKES:

HOW TO BREED: Any combination of Cold, Earth and Air Element creatures should result in a PomPom. Try to find some for yourself, but if you get stuck pairing the Tweedle and the Drumpler should produce results.

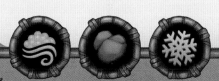

Meet the Scups!

The **SCUPS'** heavy body is filled with water. It can however stick to almost any surface with its **PLUNGER-LIKE FEET**. These feet use air to produce a call that can travel vast distances.

SPECIES: Scups

EGG:

UNLOCKED: After buying Air Island

ISLANDS: Air, Water and Gold

BEDS REQUIRED: 3

BREEDING/INCUBATION TIME: 12 hours

ELEMENTS: Air, Earth and Water

CLASS: Natural

PLACEMENT XP: 12,500

LIKES:

HOW TO BREED: Any combination of Air, Earth and Water Element monsters. One example is to pair the Tweedle and the Fwog, but there are others.

Meet the Riff!

RIFFS are masterful musicians, but very little is known about these mysterious monsters. With a distinctive look and sound, this ORANGE CREATURE plays a guitar-like instrument.

SPECIES: Riff

EGG:

UNLOCKED: After buying Air Island

ISLANDS: Air and Gold

BEDS REQUIRED: 4

BREEDING/INCUBATION TIME: 24 hours

ELEMENTS: Air, Earth, Water and Cold

CLASS: Natural

PLACEMENT ⭐: 110,000

LIKES:

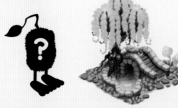

HOW TO BREED: The Riff is the 'boss' of the Air Island, meaning it is made of the four Air Island Elements – Air, Earth, Water and Cold. Combine a Double-Element monster pair like the Cybop and Maw, or for more stability try a Triple-Element and Single-Element combo, like the Scups and Mammott.

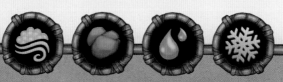

Water Island

WATER ISLAND is available for purchase for 1,500,000 Coins, but only after you have purchased AIR ISLAND. Water Island is a tranquil place, surrounded by CORAL and PEACEFUL TENTACLE CREATURES.
The monsters arrive with a SPLASH to make a JOYFUL, BUBBLY TUNE.

Monsters on this island are of the AIR, EARTH, WATER AND PLANT ELEMENTS. No COLD Element monsters can live on this island, so you cannot breed them here or purchase them from the Market.

These are the Water Island obstacles:

SMALL ROCK

COST: 2,500
XP: 2,500
CLEAR-TIME: 4 hrs
UNLOCKED: after buying island

MEDIUM ROCK

COST: 50,000
XP: 50,000
CLEAR-TIME: 16 hrs
UNLOCKED: after buying island

BIG ROCK

COST: 75,000
XP: 75,000
CLEAR-TIME: 20 hrs
UNLOCKED: after buying island

SMALL TREE

COST: 1,000
XP: 1,000
CLEAR-TIME: 2 hrs
UNLOCKED: after buying island

MEDIUM TREE

COST: 10,000
XP: 10,000
CLEAR-TIME: 8 hrs
UNLOCKED: after buying island

BIG TREE

COST: 15,000
XP: 15,000
CLEAR-TIME: 12 hrs
UNLOCKED: after buying island

Meet the Reedling!

Somewhere in their evolution **REEDLINGS** forgot how to breathe through their mouths, so they developed **FLUTE-LIKE SPINES**. They produce organ-like sounds filling the island with a **WONDERFUL MELODY**.

SPECIES: Reedling

EGG:

UNLOCKED: After buying Water Island

ISLANDS: Water, Earth and Gold

BEDS REQUIRED: 3

BREEDING/INCUBATION TIME: 12 hours

ELEMENTS: Air, Plant and Earth

CLASS: Natural

PLACEMENT XP: 11,000

LIKES:

HOW TO BREED: Any combination of Plant, Earth and Air Element creatures should result in a Reedling. Try to find some for yourself, but if you get stuck pairing the Dandidoo and the Noggin should produce results.

Meet the Shellbeat!

SHELLBEATS are shy creatures but loosen up to the sounds of their neighbouring monsters. The Shellbeat adds PERCUSSION to the island song, playing its aquatic drum set as well as its own shell.

SPECIES: Shellbeat

EGG:

UNLOCKED: After buying Water Island

ISLANDS: Water and Gold

BEDS REQUIRED: 4

BREEDING/INCUBATION
TIME: 24 hours

ELEMENTS: Air, Plant, Earth and Water

CLASS: Natural

PLACEMENT XP: 110,000

LIKES:

HOW TO BREED: The Shellbeat is the 'boss' of the Water Island, meaning it is made of the four Water Island Elements – Plant, Earth, Water and Air. Combine a Double-Element monster pair like the Dandidoo and Fwog, or for more stability try a Triple-Element and Single-Element combo, like the Scups and Potbelly.

Earth Island

EARTH ISLAND is available for purchase for 7,500,000 Coins, but only after you have purchased **WATER ISLAND**. Earth Island is humid and surrounded by molten lava, but it still provides the perfect venue for a **MONSTER ROCK PARTY!**

Monsters on this island are of the **AIR, EARTH, COLD AND PLANT ELEMENTS**. No **WATER** Element monsters can live on this island, so you cannot breed them here or purchase them from the Market.

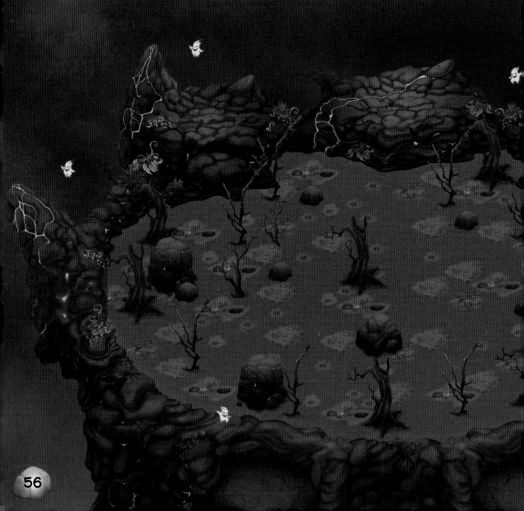

These are the Earth Island obstacles:

SMALL ROCK

COST: 10,000
XP: 10,000
CLEAR-TIME: 2 hrs
UNLOCKED: after buying island

MEDIUM ROCK

COST: 15,000
XP: 15,000
CLEAR-TIME: 12 hrs
UNLOCKED: after buying island

BIG ROCK

COST: 50,000
XP: 50,000
CLEAR-TIME: 16 hrs
UNLOCKED: after buying island

SMALL TREE

COST: 500
XP: 500
CLEAR-TIME: 10 mins
UNLOCKED: after buying island

MEDIUM TREE

COST: 2,500
XP: 2,500
CLEAR-TIME: 4 hrs
UNLOCKED: after buying island

BIG TREE

COST: 10,000
XP: 10,000
CLEAR-TIME: 8 hrs
UNLOCKED: after buying island

Meet the Quarrister!

The **QUARRISTER'S** heads are each separate creatures, banding together to harmonise and provide a wonderful chorus to the **ISLAND'S SONG**. Every once in a while one of the Quarrister's voices will go for a solo, but that kind of behaviour is usually considered to be **BiG-HEADED**.

SPECIES: Quarrister

EGG:

UNLOCKED: After buying Earth Island

ISLANDS: Earth and Gold

BEDS REQUIRED: 4

BREEDING/INCUBATION TIME: 24 hours

ELEMENTS: Air, Plant, Earth and Cold

CLASS: Natural

PLACEMENT ⭐: 110,000

LIKES:

HOW TO BREED: The Quarrister is the 'boss' of the Earth Island, meaning it is made of the four Earth Island Elements – Plant, Earth, Cold and Air. Combine a Double-Element monster pair like the Cybop and Furcorn, or for more stability try a Triple-Element and Single-Element combo, like the Reedling and Mammott.

Gold Island

GOLD ISLAND is free to access at Level 4 after you have purchased the **COLD ISLAND**. It is a special place, as you cannot purchase any monsters, decorations or structures. You cannot breed here either. The only way to fill this island is to feed up your monsters on your other islands until they reach Level 15 and then place them on Gold Island. As this island is in a **DIFFERENT DIMENSION** to your regular islands, when you place your monster on Gold Island it also remains on its original island.

All Natural Element monsters can live on Gold Island, plus Seasonals, the **WUBBOX** and Plant Island's **SHUGABUSH**. Under no circumstances can any Ethereal monsters live on Gold Island. Monsters that live here do not require feeding or decorations to make them happy. They also do not generate any Coins. The Gold Island's purpose is purely for enjoyment of the **CLASSICAL MELODY**.

Every monster dreams of one day visiting the beautiful Gold Island. Only the most experienced among them get to join its powerful song, which **CELEBRATES MONSTERS** and music of all kinds.

The Gold Island only has one type of Castle, as it has unlimited beds and therefore has no need to upgrade.

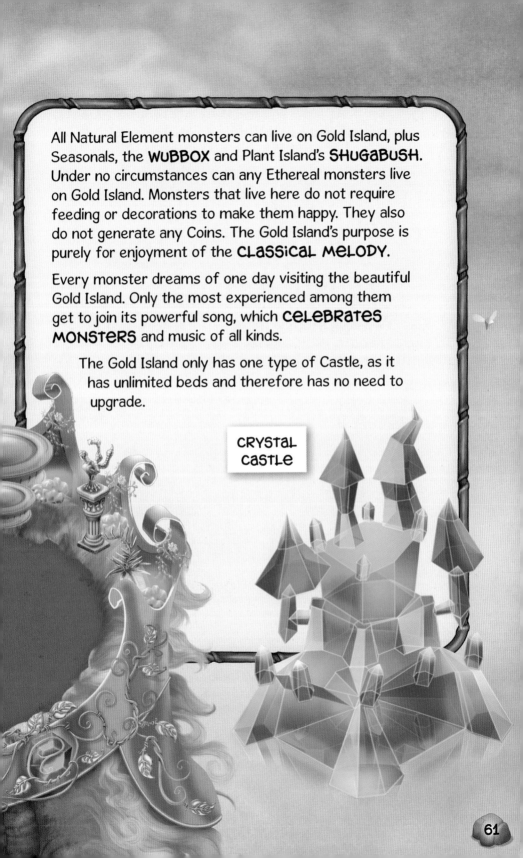

CRYSTAL CASTLE

Ethereal Island

Like the Gold Island, **ETHEREAL ISLAND** is free to access at Level 4 after you have purchased the Cold Island. Only Ethereal Element monsters can live on Ethereal Island; no Natural, Seasonal or Legendary monsters can live here.

Ethereal Island also has its own currency called **SHARDS**. These are not transferable onto any other island.

The Castle and its upgrades on Ethereal Island are much bigger than the other islands, as each Ethereal monster requires a lot more beds.

This **OTHERWORLDLY REALM** is a pocket dimension, home to mysterious creatures and substances. The song is a **WONDROUS, OMINOUS TUNE.**

THERE ARE FIVE ETHEREAL ELEMENTS:

Plasma: Shadow: Mech:

Crystal: Poison:

These are the Ethereal Island obstacles:

SMALL ROCK

COST: 4
XP: 1,750
CLEAR-TIME: 3 hrs
UNLOCKED: after getting island

MEDIUM ROCK

COST: 64
XP: 32,500
CLEAR-TIME: 14 hrs
UNLOCKED: after getting island

BIG ROCK

COST: 128
XP: 62,500
CLEAR-TIME: 18 hrs
UNLOCKED: after getting island

SMALL TREE

COST: 2
XP: 750
CLEAR-TIME: 1 hr
UNLOCKED: after getting island

MEDIUM TREE

COST: 12
XP: 6,250
CLEAR-TIME: 6 hrs
UNLOCKED: after getting island

BIG TREE

COST: 24
XP: 12,500
CLEAR-TIME: 10 hrs
UNLOCKED: after getting island

TOP TIP!
Did you know you can convert Diamonds or Coins to Shards in the Currency menu?

There are five core **ETHEREAL ELEMENT MONSTERS:**
GHAZT, GRUMPYRE, REEBRO, JEEODE and **HUMBUG.**
You cannot buy these on Ethereal Island so you need to
Teleport them from other islands. Refer to the character
profiles on the next few pages to find out where and how,
but once you have your Ethereal monster you must feed
it up to Level 15 in order to Teleport it over to Ethereal
Island. Once you have all of the core monsters you can
create any of the other 10 Ethereal Double-Element
hybrids by pairing them up in the Breeding Structure.

Even more so than the Natural
Multi-Element monsters, Ethereal
monsters are difficult to breed
successfully and may take several
tries. Make sure your monsters are
at a high level and use as many
wishing torches as
possible to get your
desired monster.

Meet the Ghazt!

The **GHAZT** is a Single-Element core Ethereal monster. It is a transparent cat-like creature with **GLOWING EYES**. To contribute to the island song, the Ghazt softly patters on five floating orbs as they rotate around it. It provides an electronic keyboard-like sound.

SPECIES: Ghazt

EGG:

UNLOCKED: Level 9

ISLANDS: Plant and Ethereal

BEDS REQUIRED: 5

BREEDING/INCUBATION TIME: 36 hours on Plant Island or 10 on Ethereal Island

ELEMENT: Plasma

CLASS: Ethereal

PLACEMENT XP : 375,000 on Plant Island or 10,125 on Ethereal Island

LIKES:

HOW TO BREED: The Ghazt can only be bred on Plant Island to begin with. To do this you need to combine one Quad-Element monster (e.g. Entbrat) and one Triple-Element monster. Try the T-Rox!

Meet the Grumpyre!

The **GRUMPYRE** resembles a bat surrounded by a cloud of black smoke. The Grumpyre repeats a chant making it easily identifiable in the island song. The Grumpyre may appear **SAD AND SCARY** but is in fact **HAPPY** and having a good time.

SPECIES: Grumpyre

EGG:

UNLOCKED: After buying Cold Island

ISLANDS: Cold and Ethereal

BEDS REQUIRED: 5

BREEDING/INCUBATION TIME: 36 hours on Cold Island or 10 on Ethereal Island

ELEMENT: Shadow

CLASS: Ethereal

PLACEMENT XP: 375,000 on Cold Island or 10,125 on Ethereal Island

LIKES:

HOW TO BREED: The Grumpyre can only be bred on Cold Island to begin with. To do this you need to combine one Quad-Element monster (Deedge) and one Triple-Element monster. Try the Spunge!

Meet the Reebro!

The **REEBRO** is a giant over-sized brain with a mechanical bug-like body. It is one of the **STRANGEST-LOOKING** monsters in the multiverse. The Reebro uses its feet to pound the ground for the beat, and emits an electric snare sound from its exhaust pipes.

SPECIES: Reebro

EGG:

UNLOCKED: After buying Air Island

ISLANDS: Air and Ethereal

BEDS REQUIRED: 5

BREEDING/INCUBATION TIME: 36 hours on Air Island or 10 on Ethereal Island

ELEMENT: Mech

CLASS: Ethereal

PLACEMENT : 375,000 on Air Island or 10,125 on Ethereal Island

Likes:

HOW TO BREED: The Reebro can only be bred on Air Island to begin with. To do this you need to combine one Quad-Element monster (Riff) and one Triple-Element monster. Try the Congle!

Meet the Jeeode!

The Jeeode is made of PINK AND ORANGE crystals. It is well-known for its ability to listen to all sides of a situation and often helps to resolve disputes between other monsters. As the Jeeode plays its prisms, it emits a magical bell sound.

SPECIES: Jeeode

EGG:

UNLOCKED: After buying Water Island

ISLANDS: Water and Ethereal

BEDS REQUIRED: 5

BREEDING/INCUBATION TIME: 36 hours on Water Island or 10 on Ethereal Island

ELEMENT: Crystal

CLASS: Ethereal

PLACEMENT XP: 375,000 on Water Island or 10,125 on Ethereal Island

LIKES:

HOW TO BREED: The Jeeode can only be bred on Water Island to begin with. To do this you need to combine one Quad-Element monster (Shellbeat) and one Triple-Element monster. Try the Pummel!

Meet the Humbug!

The **HUMBUG** resembles a bumblebee with green stripes. Humbugs naturally enjoy warm weather, and are drawn to humid places where the hum produced by their wings has the finest tone.

SPECIES: Humbug

EGG:

UNLOCKED: After buying Earth Island

ISLANDS: Earth and Ethereal

BEDS REQUIRED: 5

BREEDING/INCUBATION TIME: 36 hours on Earth Island or 10 on Ethereal Island

ELEMENT: Poison

CLASS: Ethereal

PLACEMENT : 375,000 on Earth Island or 10,125 on Ethereal Island

LIKES:

HOW TO BREED: The Humbug can only be bred on Earth Island to begin with. To do this you need to combine one Quad-Element monster (Quarrister) and one Triple-Element monster. Try the Reedling!

Meet the Nebulob!

The **NEBULOB** sings a **QUICK, QUIET AND INCOHERENT** mix of words. It is not a natural musician, but works on its sound tirelessly, experimenting with different genres and styles. The Nebulob's favourite musical genre is 'Rhythm and Ooze'.

SPECIES: Nebulob

EGG:

UNLOCKED: After getting Ethereal Island

ISLANDS: Ethereal

BEDS REQUIRED: 10

BREEDING/INCUBATION TIME: 42 hours

ELEMENTS: Plasma and Mech

CLASS: Ethereal

PLACEMENT XP: 110,000

LIKES:

HOW TO BREED: To breed a Nebulob you need a Plasma Element monster and a Mech Element monster. Combine the Ghazt and Reebro to get this alien-like creature!

Meet the Arackulele!

ARACKULELES have homemade chordophones that play rousing **MUSIC** not dissimilar to a **UKULELE**. This multi-limbed monster has an inspiring attitude towards life; believing anything is possible if enough monsters join together in harmony!

SPECIES: Arackulele

EGG:

UNLOCKED: After getting Ethereal Island

ISLANDS: Ethereal

BEDS REQUIRED: 10

BREEDING/INCUBATION TIME: 42 hours

ELEMENTS: Shadow and Mech

CLASS: Ethereal

PLACEMENT : 110,000

LIKES:

HOW TO BREED: Find a Single-Element Shadow monster and a Single-Element Mech monster to create the Arackulele. Combine the Grumpyre and Reebro to get this spider-like monster!

Meet the Whisp!

The **WHISP** sings a **SLOW AND CONSISTENT WAIL** that makes the Ethereal Island song even more mysterious. It loves to swoop and glide across the most magical island. Whisps don't cast reflections in mirrors, which makes it difficult to admire their stylish hairdos.

SPECIES: Whisp

EGG:

UNLOCKED: After getting Ethereal Island

ISLANDS: Ethereal

BEDS REQUIRED: 10

BREEDING/INCUBATION TIME: 42 hours

ELEMENTS: Plasma and Shadow

CLASS: Ethereal

PLACEMENT : 110,000

LIKES:

HOW TO BREED: To make this ghost-like creature you will need a Single-Element Plasma monster and a Single-Element Shadow monster. Try the Grumpyre and Ghazt!

Meet the Boodoo!

The **BOODOO** has a menacing appearance but is actually a **CREATIVE AND GENTLE CREATURE**. It produces a maraca sound with its **CRYSTAL SHAKERS,** which it makes itself. It is famed for its artistic pursuits; monsters will travel from far and wide to witness the unveiling of a Boodoo original.

SPECIES: Boodoo

EGG:

UNLOCKED: After getting the Ethereal Island

ISLANDS: Ethereal

BEDS REQUIRED: 10

BREEDING/INCUBATION TIME: 42 hours

ELEMENTS: Shadow and Crystal

CLASS: Ethereal

PLACEMENT : 110,000

LIKES:

HOW TO BREED: The Boodoo can be bred using a Shadow Element and a Crystal Element monster. Add the Grumpyre and Jeeode together to get this imaginative monster!

Meet the Sox!

The Sox has **GAPING HOLES** in its tail, which it fills with metal pads by eating precious stones. It uses these pads, along with its **LONG SNOUT**, to create **MUSICAL RIFFS**, not unlike a saxophone. The age-old mystery of 'what does the Sox say?' has now been solved.

SPECIES: Sox

EGG:

UNLOCKED: After getting Ethereal Island

ISLANDS: Ethereal

BEDS REQUIRED: 10

BREEDING/INCUBATION TIME: 42 hours

ELEMENTS: Plasma and Crystal

CLASS: Ethereal

PLACEMENT XP: 110,000

LIKES:

HOW TO BREED: Combine the Jeeode, a Crystal Element monster, and the Ghazt, a Plasma Element monster, to get this jazzy creature!

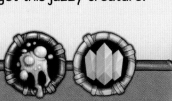

Meet the Kazilleon!

The **KAZILLEON** is a reptilian monster with four arms and two legs. These monsters are **NOTORIOUSLY SMELLY** – the fumes from their mouths have been known to singe fur. But these bass-singing creatures are so friendly they are kept around anyway.

SPECIES: Kazilleon

EGG:

UNLOCKED: After getting Etheral Island

ISLANDS: Ethereal

BEDS REQUIRED: 10

BREEDING/INCUBATION TIME: 42 hours

ELEMENTS: Shadow and Poison

CLASS: Ethereal

PLACEMENT XP: 110,000

LIKES:

HOW TO BREED: Combine a Single-Element Shadow monster and a Single-Element Poison monster to create the Kazilleon. Try the Grumpyre and Humbug!

Meet the Bellowfish!

BELLOWFiSH are natives to the aquaslime pools of Ethereal Island, but have developed **MECHANICAL SUITS** powered by crystals, which allow them to breathe out of water. They have **LONG, SPRiNGY ARMS** that move about to produce an accordion-like sound.

SPECIES: Bellowfish

EGG:

UNLOCKED: After getting Ethereal Island

ISLANDS: Ethereal

BEDS REQUIRED: 10

BREEDiNG/INCUBATION TiME: 42 hours

ELEMENTS: Mech and Crystal

CLASS: Ethereal

PLACEMENT XP: 110,000

LiKES:

HOW TO BREED: Add a Mech Element monster to a Crystal Element monster to get a Bellowfish. Combine the Reebro and Jeeode to get this fishy monster!

Meet the Dragong!

The **DRAGONG** has **CYMBALS FOR FEET** and three more on its tail. These plates produce a **GONG-LIKE RINGING** when the creature stomps its feet and wiggles its tail, and allow the Dragong to skim the water.

SPECIES: Dragong

EGG:

UNLOCKED: After getting Ethereal Island

ISLANDS: Ethereal

BEDS REQUIRED: 10

BREEDING/INCUBATION TIME: 42 hours

ELEMENTS: Mech and Poison

CLASS: Ethereal

PLACEMENT XP: 110,000

LIKES:

HOW TO BREED: Combine the Reebro, a Single-Element Mech monster, and the Humbug, a Single-Element Poison monster, to get this dragon-like monster!

Meet the Jellbilly!

JELLBILLIES are legends to the scavenging Cybops of the neighbouring dimension. Their song is modelled after the Jellbilly's own VOCAL TWANG. The Jellbilly's unusual fins and face-tentacles resemble a STETSON AND A MOUSTACHE.

SPECIES: Jellbilly

EGG:

UNLOCKED: After getting Ethereal Island

ISLANDS: Ethereal

BEDS REQUIRED: 10

BREEDING/INCUBATION TIME: 42 hours

ELEMENTS: Plasma and Poison

CLASS: Ethereal

PLACEMENT XP: 110,000

LIKES:

HOW TO BREED: To breed the floating Jellbilly, you will need a Poison Element and a Plasma Element monster combo. Try the Humbug and Ghazt!

Meet the Fung Pray!

The **FUNG PRAY** resembles a praying mantis with a mushroom headcap. This **TRANQUIL MONSTER** strives to create balance in its life and uses its arms to produce high-pitched **VIOLIN SOUNDS**.

SPECIES: Fung Pray

EGG:

UNLOCKED: After getting Ethereal Island

ISLANDS: Ethereal

BEDS REQUIRED: 10

BREEDING/INCUBATION TIME: 42 hours

ELEMENTS: Crystal and Poison

CLASS: Ethereal

PLACEMENT XP: 110,000

LIKES:

HOW TO BREED: Combine the Crystal Element Jeeode and the Poison Element Humbug to get this zen monster!

Shugabush Island

The **SHUGABUSH ISLAND** is also available for free at Level 4, once you have purchased the Air Island. Some Natural monsters can live here, **BUT NO ETHEREAL MONSTERS** can be bred or bought here. The Shugabush community is partly made up of creatures of the **LEGENDARY CLASS**.

The Castle on Shugabush Island does not produce a bass sound like the Natural Island Castles do.

The Legendary **SHUGABUSH MONSTER** supervises this island, leading it in a musical experience never heard before. The Shugabush monsters produce a **CATCHY ROCK TUNE** with their instruments and **SMOOTH VOICES**. Collectively they are known as the **SHUGAFAM**.

These are the Shugabush Island obstacles:

SMALL ROCK

COST: 2,500
XP: 2,500
CLEAR-TIME: 3 hrs
UNLOCKED: after getting island

MEDIUM ROCK

COST: 50,000
XP: 50,000
CLEAR-TIME: 14 hrs
UNLOCKED: after getting island

BIG ROCK

COST: 75,000
XP: 75,000
CLEAR-TIME: 18 hrs
UNLOCKED: after getting island

SMALL TREE

COST: 1,000
XP: 1,000
CLEAR-TIME: 1 hr
UNLOCKED: after getting island

MEDIUM TREE

COST: 10,000
XP: 10,000
CLEAR-TIME: 6 hrs
UNLOCKED: after getting island

BIG TREE

COST: 15,000
XP: 15,000
CLEAR-TIME: 10 hrs
UNLOCKED: after getting island

Breeding on Shugabush Island

The **SHUGABUSH** monster is essential to all breeding on Shugabush Island. Refer to the character profiles on the next few pages to find out where and how, but once you have a Shugabush on your island, you need to add **NATURAL** monsters for it to breed with.

The following Natural monsters can live on **SHUGABUSH ISLAND**:

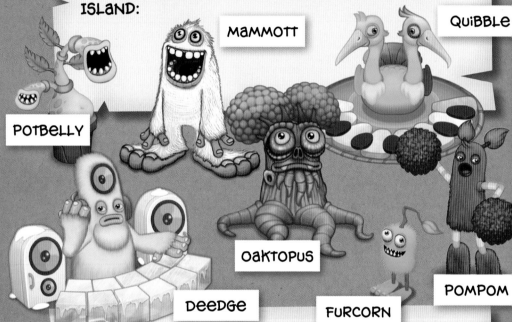

MAMMOTT

QUIBBLE

POTBELLY

OAKTOPUS

DEEDGE

FURCORN

POMPOM

You will need all of these to create the complete Shugabush band. To introduce these Natural monsters to Shugabush Island you need to feed them up to Level 15 and then **TELEPORT THEM**. Once you choose to Teleport a monster to Shugabush Island it will be removed from its current island, and also from Gold Island if it also exists there.

Like the Ethereal monsters, Shugafam monsters are **DIFFICULT TO BREED** successfully and may take several tries. Make sure your monsters are at a high level, and use as many **WISHING TORCHES** as possible to get your desired monster.

Meet the Shugabush!

Never seen without its hat, the **SHUGABUSH** is a skilled performer. It has long twiggy fingers that allow it to easily pluck the strings of its **TREASURED MANDOLIN**. The Shugabush sometimes sings along if the mood strikes it.

SPECIES: Shugabush

EGG:

UNLOCKED: Level 9

ISLANDS: Plant, Gold and Shugabush

BEDS REQUIRED: 2

BREEDING/INCUBATION TIME: 35 hours

ELEMENT: Legendary

CLASS: Legendary

PLACEMENT : 50,000

LIKES:

HOW TO BREED: To breed the cheerful Shugabush, you need to head over to Plant Island and combine the Bowgart with the Clamble. Then feed your Shugabush up to Level 15 and Teleport it to Shugabush Island. Or leave it on Plant Island to jam with its leafy pals.

Meet the Shugabass!

This **COOL CUSTOMER** delivers a mean bass line with electric bass guitar. **THE SHUGABASS'S** pelt is the perfect environment for a special fungus to thrive, which gives it its **DISTINCT TEAL COLOUR.**

SPECIES: Shugabass

EGG:

UNLOCKED: After getting Shugabush Island

ISLANDS: Shugabush

BEDS REQUIRED: 3

BREEDING/INCUBATION TIME: 35 hours

ELEMENT: Legendary

CLASS: Legendary

PLACEMENT XP: 50,000

LIKES:

HOW TO BREED: The Shugabass is a result of pairing the Shugabush with the Potbelly.

Meet the Shugitar!

The **SHUGITAR'S** coat is a **MUDDY BROWN,** matching its guitar. It is still an excellent musician despite its tendency to blend in with the Shugabush Island background. The Shugitar's **GUITAR RIFF** plays side-by-side with the Shugavox's singing.

SPECIES: Shugitar

EGG:

UNLOCKED: After getting Shugabush Island

ISLANDS: Shugabush

BEDS REQUIRED: 3

BREEDING/INCUBATION TIME: 35 hours

ELEMENT: Legendary

CLASS: Legendary

PLACEMENT : 50,000

LIKES:

HOW TO BREED: Combine the Shugabush with the PomPom to create the Shugitar.

Meet the Shugajo!

The **SHUGAJO** has daily mudbaths to soothe the mind and keep the limbs limber. The Shugafam **VALUES PRECISION** above all else, so the Shugajo is master of an instrument that requires a **FINELY-HONED TECHNIQUE**. It plays its banjo beautifully in time with the Shugabush.

SPECIES: Shugajo

EGG:

UNLOCKED: After getting Shugabush Island

ISLANDS: Shugabush

BEDS REQUIRED: 3

BREEDING/INCUBATION TIME: 35 hours

ELEMENT: Legendary

CLASS: Legendary

PLACEMENT XP: 50,000

LIKES:

HOW TO BREED: Pairing the Shugabush with the Oaktopus can result in the Shugajo.

Meet the Shugarock!

The **SHUGAROCK** loves nothing more than to kick back and relax when it is not strumming its guitar. Very similar to the Shugabush except for its **BRILLIANT BLUE GUITAR,** this Legendary monster provides a rising guitar riff that really **LIVENS UP** the Shugafam sound.

SPECIES: Shugarock

EGG:

UNLOCKED: After getting Shugabush Island

ISLANDS: Shugabush

BEDS REQUIRED: 3

BREEDING/INCUBATION TIME: 35 hours

ELEMENT: Legendary

CLASS: Legendary

PLACEMENT XP: 50,000

LIKES:

HOW TO BREED: The Shugarock is created by breeding the Shugabush with the Mammott.

Meet the Shugabuzz!

The **SHUGABUZZ** is the most eccentric member of the Shugafam with its vibrant **TOP HAT** and facial fur stylings. It plays a strange guitar-like instrument that emits an electric **BUZZING SOUND**.

SPECIES: Shugabuzz

EGG:

UNLOCKED: After getting Shugabush Island

ISLANDS: Shugabush

BEDS REQUIRED: 3

BREEDING/INCUBATION TIME: 35 hours

ELEMENT: Legendary

CLASS: Legendary

PLACEMENT XP: 50,000

LIKES:

HOW TO BREED: Add the Quibble and the Shugabush together to get a Shugabuzz.

Meet the Shugabeats!

The **SHUGaBEaTS** is an accomplished gardener, growing different types of **MUSHROOMS** to use in its drum kit. It keeps the **ViTaL BeaT** of the Shugabush Island.

SPECiES: Shugabeats

EGG:

UNLOCKED: After getting Shugabush Island

ISLaNDS: Shugabush

BEDS REQUiRED: 3

BREEDiNG/INCUBATiON TiME: 35 hours

ELEMENT: Legendary

CLASS: Legendary

PLaCEMENT : 50,000

LiKES:

HOW TO BREED: Try partnering a Shugabush with a Furcorn to make a Shugabeats.

Meet the Shugavox!

The **SHUGAVOX** loves to wail a wild tune. It has a friendly rivalry with the Shugabush, competing to see who has the best **HAT, SCARF** and who's the **BETTER MUSICIAN.**

SPECIES: Shugavox

EGG:

UNLOCKED: After getting Shugabush Island

ISLANDS: Shugabush

BEDS REQUIRED: 3

BREEDING/INCUBATION TIME: 35 hours

ELEMENT: Legendary

CLASS: Legendary

PLACEMENT XP: 50,000

LIKES:

HOW TO BREED: Join the Deedge and the Shugabush together to gain a Shugavox.

Meet the Wubbox!

One day, as the monsters were tunnelling underground, they stumbled upon an IMMENSE UNDERGROUND VAULT containing several of the mysterious objects known as the WUBBOX.

SPECIES: Wubbox

EGG:

UNLOCKED: Level 20

ISLANDS: Plant, Cold, Air, Water, Earth, Gold and Ethereal

BEDS REQUIRED: 6

BREEDING/INCUBATION TIME: 48 hours

ELEMENT: Electricity

CLASS: Supernatural

PLACEMENT XP: 37,500,000

LIKES:

HOW TO BREED: The Wubbox cannot be bred, only purchased from the Market.

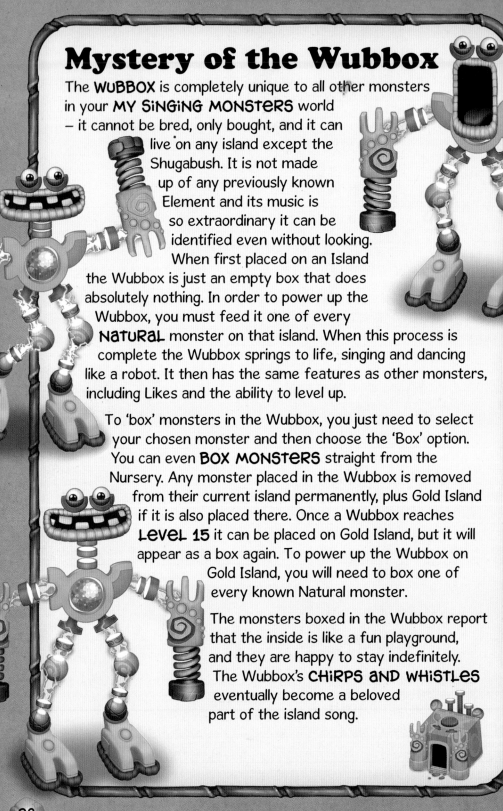

Mystery of the Wubbox

The **WUBBOX** is completely unique to all other monsters in your **MY SiNGiNG MONSTERS** world – it cannot be bred, only bought, and it can live on any island except the Shugabush. It is not made up of any previously known Element and its music is so extraordinary it can be identified even without looking. When first placed on an Island the Wubbox is just an empty box that does absolutely nothing. In order to power up the Wubbox, you must feed it one of every **NaTuRaL** monster on that island. When this process is complete the Wubbox springs to life, singing and dancing like a robot. It then has the same features as other monsters, including Likes and the ability to level up.

To 'box' monsters in the Wubbox, you just need to select your chosen monster and then choose the 'Box' option. You can even **BOX MONSTERS** straight from the Nursery. Any monster placed in the Wubbox is removed from their current island permanently, plus Gold Island if it is also placed there. Once a Wubbox reaches **LeVeL 15** it can be placed on Gold Island, but it will appear as a box again. To power up the Wubbox on Gold Island, you will need to box one of every known Natural monster.

The monsters boxed in the Wubbox report that the inside is like a fun playground, and they are happy to stay indefinitely. The Wubbox's **CHiRPS aND WHiSTLeS** eventually become a beloved part of the island song.

Seasonal Monsters

There are a few monsters which are only available during a short window of time for breeding or purchasing. The exact dates are different year to year, but the island the monster is found on will be decorated differently when the opportunity to breed these monsters is possible. The Seasonal monsters are:

PUNKLETON – available at Halloween on the Plant Island. The Plant Island is decorated in ghoulish attire.

YOOL – available at Christmas on the Cold Island. The Cold Island is decorated in festive gear.

SCHMOOCHLE – available at Valentine's on the Air Island. The Air Island has heart-shaped balloons and is strewn with candy hearts.

BLABBIT – available at Easter on the Water Island. The Water Island is covered with painted eggs and strange sculptures.

HOOLA – available during the summer on Earth Island. The Earth Island is decorated with tropical fruit and tiki torches.

Meet the Punkleton!

The **PUNKLETON** lies low most of the year, with only its head poking above the soil. For a limited time it will wrench itself out of the ground to **SCARE THE OTHER MONSTERS** with its unruly tune.

SPECIES: Punkleton

EGG:

UNLOCKED: Level 9

ISLANDS: Plant and Gold

BEDS REQUIRED: 1

BREEDING/INCUBATION TIME: 18 hours

ELEMENTS: None

CLASS: Seasonal

PLACEMENT XP: 110,000

LIKES:

HOW TO BREED: The Punkleton is available to breed during Halloween when the Plant Island is decorated accordingly. Pair the Bowgart with the T-Rox for this Seasonal monster.

Meet the Yool!

The **YOOL** waits for the end of the year to visit the Cold Island, just in time for the festive season. Its arrival is heralded by jingle bells and feelings of joy spread throughout the land. The other monsters invite the Yool to stay year-round, but this monster only provides its booming voice once a year.

SPECIES: Yool

EGG:

UNLOCKED: After buying Cold Island

ISLANDS: Cold and Gold

BEDS REQUIRED: 1

BREEDING/INCUBATION TIME: 36 hours

ELEMENTS: None

CLASS: Seasonal

PLACEMENT XP: 110,000

LIKES:

HOW TO BREED: Yool is available in the lead up to Christmas. Pair a Deedge with the Congle for this festive monster.

Meet the Schmoochle!

The two-headed **SCHMOOCHLE** is a mystery – some believe two individual monsters fell in love and merged, but others insist it was born this way. Either way, its **ROMANTIC DUET** is a welcome addition to Air Island.

SPECIES: Schmoochle

EGG:

UNLOCKED: After buying Air Island

ISLANDS: Air and Gold

BEDS REQUIRED: 2

BREEDING/INCUBATION TIME: 31 hours

ELEMENTS: None

CLASS: Seasonal

PLACEMENT XP: 110,000

LIKES:

HOW TO BREED: The Schmoochle is available in February. Combine the Tweedle and the Riff for this harmonizing monster.

Meet the Blabbit!

The **BLABBIT** blows bubbles when it breathes, making delightful trilling sounds as it does so. The Blabbit has a reputation for causing trouble by borrowing monster eggs and hiding them around the island, but it is too cute to stay mad at.

SPECIES: Blabbit

EGG:

UNLOCKED: After buying Water Island

ISLANDS: Water and Gold

BEDS REQUIRED: 1

BREEDING/INCUBATION TIME: 19 hours

ELEMENTS: None

CLASS: Seasonal

PLACEMENT XP: 110,000

LIKES:

HOW TO BREED: The Blabbit is an Easter time monster created by pairing the Scups with the Spunge.

Meet the Hoola!

The **HOOLA** is often mistaken for a PomPom that has switched to yellow foods. But it is a unique creature with a distinct look and sound. The Hoola loves playing pranks on other monsters and getting into trouble whenever possible.

SPECIES: Hoola

EGG:

UNLOCKED: After buying Air Island

ISLANDS: Air, Earth and Gold

BEDS REQUIRED: 1

BREEDING/INCUBATION TIME: 25 hours

ELEMENTS: None

CLASS: Seasonal

PLACEMENT XP: 110,000

LIKES:

HOW TO BREED: The Hoola is available for one month in summer. Add a Pango and a PomPom to the Breeding Structure to achieve this dazzling monster.

Now you have learned about
all of the monsters, all the islands and
some top game tips available in
MY SiNGING MONSTERS
you are ready to create musical, colourful islands
full of unique creatures.

Enjoy!